Happy 12th Birthday

Made in the USA
Middletown, DE
12 November 2019

78526577R00066